C000225742

The Power of the 60s

Only four months old, Construction-subsector No 60 095 *Crib Goch* stands at the head of a train of wagons being loaded at Swinden Quarry, near Grassington, on 30 July 1992. *Gavin Morrison*

094

The Power of the 60s

Gavin Morrison

An imprint of
Ian Allan Publishing

Contents

Frontispiece:
On 24 April 1993 trains were diverted from the West Coast main line via the Settle & Carlisle, and in a most unusual occurrence, No 60 094 *Tryfan* of the Construction subsector worked south on its own with train 1M02, the 09.24 Edinburgh–Birmingham. Piloting Class 47/4 No 47 973, it returned north on the down 'Royal Scot', seen leaving Gisburn Tunnel *en route* for Hellifield. *Gavin Morrison*

Half-title page:
Prior to construction of the Class 60s Brush made a model of the proposed design, seen here in grey livery with Railfreight 'general user' decals. *Brush Traction*

First published 2007

ISBN (10) 0 86093 609 0
ISBN (13) 978 0 86093 609 1

Published by Oxford Publishing Co

an imprint of Ian Allan Publishing Ltd, Hersham, Surrey, KT12 4RG
Printed in England by Ian Allan Printing Ltd, Hersham, Surrey, KT12 4RG

Code: 0710/B1

Visit the Ian Allan Publishing website at www.ianallanpublishing.com

Introduction

The arrival in the UK in January 1986 of four Class 59 locomotives, built for the Foster Yeoman quarry company, was to have a profound influence on the motive-power situation for freight in Britain. They were built by General Motors at La Grange, Illinois, USA, to haul the heavy Foster Yeoman trains, and BR's Railfreight Sector was quick to realise that their performance for heavy-haul work was infinitely superior to that its own Type 5 locomotives of Classes 56 and 58, which were mainly confined to the Coal subsector.

It was the Petroleum subsector that approached the British Railways Board about buying 20 Class 59s, which would allow the elimination of double-heading by Classes 31 and 37 on the subsector's heavy trains, as well as reducing the need for Class 47s; it was claimed that operating costs would be greatly reduced, as would fuel bills, and better reliability would be achieved.

The other Trainload subsectors quickly put in claims with the Board for similar numbers, and by mid-1987 a requirement for 100 locomotives had been identified. This requirement was put out to competitive tender, and three companies expressed an interest: Metro-Cammell, Brush and an American consortium. Metro-Cammell soon dropped out, and things moved quickly until in May 1988 an order was placed with Brush, based on what was believed to be the best and most cost-effective specification; however, with it came very tight deadlines and warranty terms. Brush being a British company, this was considered a great achievement for the locomotive-building industry, although, as history was to show, the conditions agreed by Brush, particularly the time-scale, were to cause terrible problems.

Brush's Falcon Works at Loughborough was to be the main assembly point, and the bodyshells were constructed and painted by Procor. The bodies were delivered by road and became a common sight travelling south on the M1 motorway. The Mirrlees 3,100hp 8MB275T engines were built in Stockport, and the alternators were built by Brush.

The selling points for the locomotives included reduced fuel consumption, reduced noise, and reduced maintenance costs. They would achieve 4,000 TOPS hours (equivalent to 80,000 miles) per annum, with major overhauls every 7½ years; it was claimed that the maintenance costs would be a third that of a Class 56 or 58. One of the advanced features was SEPEX, which

Right:
A comparison of front-end liveries on 2 June 2006: on the left is No 60 060 *James Watt*, still showing the Coal-subsector decal (to the rear of the cab door) on its Railfreight grey livery, while on the right, in EWS colours, is No 60 041, originally named *High Willhays*. *Gavin Morrison*

detects slipping of individual traction motors, thus minimising wheel slip. This feature was also available on the Class 59s, but was technically different from and, in theory, not as advanced as that fitted to the Class 60s. New two-pack paint was used, which has certainly stood the test of time, as some of the locomotives have never been repainted for, in some cases, around 16 to 17 years, and when cleaned still look reasonable.

No 60 001 was delivered on time on 30 June 1989 with due ceremony, during which those in attendance no doubt congratulated themselves on a job well done. It passed into the hands of the Railway Technical Centre at Derby, and was sent to the Mickleover test track. Construction at Loughborough continued quickly, but unfortunately major problems developed during testing, mainly to do with software, but also with the suspension, as well as other minor faults. It soon became clear that Brush had not really been given enough time to test the features, and had committed itself to unrealistic schedules.

Modification after modification was deemed essential, yet construction was continuing at a fast rate. The latest engines off the production line had the modifications incorporated, while earlier units were not accepted into traffic until they had received them. Consequently the yards at the factory were full of new Class 60s awaiting modification (see page 10). The result was that delivery-into-traffic schedules were severely disrupted, and training schedules for both technical and driving staff were badly delayed. The terms of the contract stipulated that a locomotive had to carry out 1,000 trouble-free hours of running before being accepted, presumably with all the modifications carried out. No 60 015 was the last to be accepted into service, on 24 March 1993, around three years after it was completed. The management of the Trainload Freight subsectors were not at all happy, and the class thus began its career under a cloud; to add insult to injury, the locomotives did not achieve the promised availability, and fuel consumption was poorer than anticipated.

However, the class eventually settled down and, whilst they did not deliver everything expected of them, their haulage capabilities were in no doubt. Even today there are many EWS diagrams, particularly petroleum trains, that require Class 60 haulage.

The '60s' have the dubious distinction of being the last heavy-freight locomotives built in this country to date, and unfortunately this may remain the situation for ever. When EWS decided it wanted 250 new locomotives, there were no doubt people still around who remembered the introduction of the Class 60s, and were also probably aware of how the Class 59s arrived and worked virtually from day one, which probably accounts for the fact that today's rail freight companies almost all employ Class 66s, built by General Motors in Ontario, Canada.

Above:
No 60 017 *Shotton Works Centenary Year 1996* heads north along the single-track goods line over Sharnbrook Summit, between Bedford and Wellingborough, with train 6F93, the King's Cross–Ketton empty cement tanks, in August 2003. Until August 1996 this locomotive had been named *Arenig Fawr*. *J. Turner*

Below:
Having just uncoupled from the wagons of the 6M17 10.18 Leeds Stourton–Peak Forest train of 9 June 2006, Loadhaul-liveried No 60 059 *Swinden Dalesman* sets off for the stabling point at Peak Forest. *Gavin Morrison*

Of late there has been much speculation in the railway press regarding the future of the Class 60s, but if EWS decides to dispense with their services it will need something with better haulage capabilities than the standard Class 66. It might be possible to re-engine them, but at what cost?

It is probably fair to say that there are a few members of the class that will never run again in their present form. The number in service varies from month to month, in the summer dropping to around 20 or 30. As far as it is known no major overhauls are currently being carried out, so some locomotives must have high engine hours.

The Class 60s have received a lot of attention from enthusiasts, no doubt due to the wide variety of liveries they have carried.

I hope I have managed in this book to tell the story behind the Class 60s, from construction to the summer months of 2007, and I personally hope that they will be around for some time to come, to break the dominance of the Class 66s.

I should like to express my particular thanks to Phil Norris at Brush, for his help in providing the construction pictures; also to my friends, for helping to fill a few gaps around the country where my coverage of the class was incomplete. Once again I have enjoyed putting this album together, and I hope that readers feel that I have managed adequately to portray the Class 60s at work.

Gavin Morrison
Mirfield
August 2007

Bibliography

The Allocation History of BR Diesels & Electrics, Volumes 3 and 6, compiled by Roger Harris and published by the author in 2003 and 2006.
Rail magazine (various issues), published by EMAP.

Construction

Right:
The bodyshells were manufactured by Procor at Horbury, near Wakefield, and were delivered by road already painted; one is seen here arriving at the works. Procor was subsequently taken over by Bombardier and used for the assembly of the Virgin 'Voyagers' but has recently been closed.
Brush Traction

Left:
An unidentified bodyshell in the early stages of assembly in the erecting shop at Brush.
Brush Traction

Right:
No 60 034 in the early stages of assembly on 30 May 1990.
Brush Traction

Left:
Cab notices inside No 60 077, photographed on 23 October 1991.
Brush Traction

Above:
Nos 60 091/089/092/093/090 in various stages of assembly inside the erecting shop on 25 October 1991.
Brush Traction

Right:
This impressive picture, no doubt taken from the overhead crane in the erecting shop, shows seven members of the class under construction towards the end of 1990. Nos 60 045 and 60 046 can be identified on the left.
Brush Traction

Above:
Another overhead view, showing an unidentified member of the class with its new Mirrlees engine installed. *Brush Traction*

Right:
No 60 013, with its *Robert Boyle* nameplate attached and bearing Petroleum subsector decals, receives a final check-over before starting acceptance trials. It would be accepted by British Rail on 29 January 1993, a considerable time after completion, following the incorporation of modifications developed as a result of the trials. *Brush Traction*

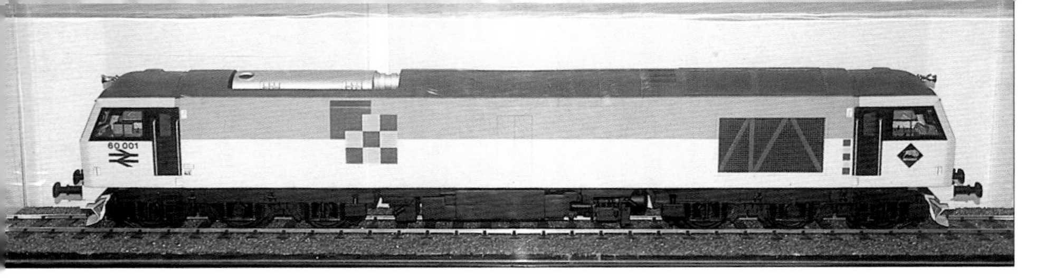

Above:
Bassett-Lowke built this model of No 60 001 for Brush, with Construction subsector decals but no name. *Gavin Morrison*

Below:
No 60 001 was allocated the name *Steadfast*. An extra nameplate was cast for Brush and is displayed in the company's offices. *Gavin Morrison*

Right:
Mike Frampton, Class 60 Project Manager (left), with Derek Cooke, the Brush Project Representative. *Brush Traction*

Below:
At least 10 members of the class can be seen in the yard at Brush Traction on 4 June 1990. The locomotives are complete but are awaiting the various modifications that became necessary as a result of trials. They did not enter service in numerical order. On the left (front to back) are Nos 60 022/024/025, concealing another, unidentified example. Standing alone is No 60 015, next to No 60 018 in front of another locomotive. On the right are Nos 60 021/020/019. *N. Stead collection*

On Trial

Right:
The completed No 60 001 *Steadfast* on the Mickleover test track on 13 July 1989. *N. Stead collection*

Above:
Early Class 60s underwent extensive testing which showed up many faults, especially with the software, causing considerable delays before Trainload Freight would accept any locomotives. Here No 60 001 *Steadfast* leaves Tyne Yard on a test train, the 6Z25 Mountsorrel–Inverness, on 7 June 1990. *N. Stead collection*

Right:
No 60 003 *Christopher Wren*, with Petroleum decals, passes Finningley while on test, believed to be heading to Immingham, on 1 August 1990; it would be 16 months before it was accepted into service. *N. Stead collection*

Right:
Also on trial, the Petroleum subsector's No 60 002 *Capability Brown* sets off past Ouston Junction with train 6Z25, the Mountsorrel–Inverness Redland wagons, on 8 June 1990. *N. Stead collection*

Left:
No 60 007 *Robert Adam* passes Pelaw Junction with a Tyne-Tees test working on 20 July 1990. Not until 5 February 1993 would this locomotive be accepted into service. *N. Stead collection*

Below:
An early working over the Settle & Carlisle line sees No 60 006 *Great Gable* heading north past Waitby during trials on 31 August 1990. It would be accepted into traffic on 23 April 1991. *N. Stead collection*

Right:
In June 1990 Nos 60 002 *Capability Brown* and 60 001 *Steadfast* were tested on the Highland main line between Inverness and Aviemore, hauling Redland wagons. With 15 miles to go to the summit at Slochd (1,315ft), including 6 miles at 1 in 60, the train is seen heading south on 10 June, having just crossed the magnificent viaduct at Culloden. *J. Turner*

Below:
With test coach No 6 coupled between them the pair are seen again at Slochd Summit, heading north after tackling the 5-mile climb at 1 in 60/92/70 from Carr Bridge. *J. Turner*

Locomotive Portraits

Left:
Production of the Class 60s, at Brush's Falcon Works, commenced in January 1989 with No **60 001**, which was completed by June of that year. Testing was carried out until the end of 1990, when, named *Steadfast*, the locomotive entered service with Railfreight's Construction subsector. It is seen here in original condition, heading south past Wandsworth Road with a hopper train on 16 September 1996. *Brian Stephenson*

Left:
Named *Capability Brown* at the start of its career in August 1989, No **60 002** was used for testing purposes until around October 1990. Originally allocated to the Petroleum subsector, it is shown here on coal duties at Monk Fryston and heads west with an empty 'merry-go-round' (MGR) train on 6 May 1994. *Gavin Morrison*

Right:
Completed on 22 July 1989, No **60 003** was not actually taken into BR stock until December 1992. In the meantime it was used for crew training, being based at Old Oak Common, Immingham, Healey Mills and Crewe. Still with its original *Christopher Wren* nameplates (since removed), it is shown in Petroleum subsector livery outside the depot at Healey Mills on a wintry 11 February 1991. *Gavin Morrison*

Right:
First of the class to be allocated to the Coal subsector was No **60 004**, named *Lochnagar*. Before entering regular service it spent nearly two years on crew training and at the Railway Technical Centre at Derby. Here it is heading an up gypsum train from Newbiggin to Drax past Settle Junction on 18 November 1994. *Gavin Morrison*

Right:
Originally named *Skiddaw*, No **60 005** had the distinction of being the first member of the class to haul a revenue-earning train, on 11 December 1989. It is seen here in charge of the 6M68 Dewsbury–Earle's Sidings cement, emerging from the deep cutting at Horbury, just to the east of Healey Mills yard, on 15 August 1995. By this time in Transrail livery, it was originally allocated to the Metals subsector. *Gavin Morrison*

Left:
Originally named *Great Gable* and allocated to the Construction subsector, No **60 006** became a favourite with enthusiasts from 1997, when it was painted in the attractive blue livery of British Steel, being renamed *Scunthorpe Ironmaster* at a press launch at Frodingham on 17 July. Here, on 6 November 1999, it is hauling a Port Talbot–Llanwern ore train past St Brides, on the main line between Cardiff and Newport. Along with No 60 033 it would later be repainted in the silver livery of Corus. *Gavin Morrison*

Left:
No **60 007** *Robert Adam* was completed by the end of December 1989 but was not actually taken into stock, with the Petroleum subsector, until February 1993, having been used extensively for training. One of five members of the class to receive the distinctive Loadhaul livery, it is seen here on 19 September 1998 passing Langstone Rock, near Dawlish, with the Burngullow–Irvine china-clay tanks, which train it would work as far as Newport. *Gavin Morrison*

Right:
Completed at Brush in January 1990, No **60 008** *Moel Fammau* was used for training before being accepted into traffic with the Metals subsector on 8 December 1992. Renamed *Gypsum Queen II* at Kirkby Thore on 27 September 1995, it is seen in Loadhaul livery at the head of a train of MGR wagons at Carstairs on 29 July 1998. *Gavin Morrison*

Above:
In immaculate external condition in EWS livery, No **60 009** takes the Derby line at Clay Cross Junction *en route* from Lackenby to Llanwern with a train of steel slabs. This locomotive was another initially used for training, having been completed around the end of 1989 but not being taken into stock until 11 February 1993, when it entered traffic with the Construction subsector. Erroneously named *Bow Fell* by Brush, it had this corrected to its intended name, *Carnedd Dafydd*, in February 1990. However, it lost its nameplates in March 1997 and was thus nameless by the time this photograph was taken on 21 August 2004. *Gavin Morrison*

Right:
Having reversed at Warrington Arpley with a train of empty MGR wagons from Fiddler's Ferry power station, No **60 010**, with EWS branding, sets off for the yard at Warrington on 11 May 2002. Originally allocated to the Petroleum subsector, it carried one nameplate in Welsh and one in English (*Pumlumon / Plynlimon*), but these were removed in February 1997. *Gavin Morrison*

Left:
Originally named *Cader Idris*, No **60 011** entered traffic on 11 October 1991, working from Toton and allocated to the Construction subsector at Leicester. It eventually became part of the Mainline fleet and was one of three Class 60s (Nos 60 011/044/078) to be painted in the attractive blue livery. Initially the trio were seldom seen away from Southern England, but with the emergence of EWS they became more widely travelled. No 60 011 is seen approaching Brocklesby, near Immingham, with an 'Enterprise' service from Doncaster on 16 June 2003.
Gavin Morrison

Right:
Accepted into traffic on 22 November 1991, No **60 012** was allocated to the Construction subsector at Leicester. It was named *Glyder Fawr*, although the plates were removed in August 1996, when it became one of the first of the class to receive EWS livery. On 15 May 1997 it was heading north on the Birmingham–Bristol main line with a Westerleigh–Robston tank train; this picture was taken at Standish Junction, south of Cheltenham, where the former Great Western route to Swindon (left) diverges. *Gavin Morrison*

Right:
Accepted into traffic on 29 January 1993 and allocated to the Petroleum subsector, No **60 013** *Robert Boyle* had lost all its decals by 17 March 2003, when it was photographed heading west past Eastleigh at the head of train 7O39, the 08.36 Merehead–Hamworthy stone train.
Jason Rogers

Right:
Having entered service on 6 January 1993, No **60 014** *Alexander Fleming* was still running with Petroleum subsector decals and with namplates *in situ* when photographed passing Mauds Bridge, between Scunthorpe and Stainforth, with a loaded Humber–Rectory tank train on 13 April 2004. *Gavin Morrison*

Right:
Completed in February 1990, No **60 015** was not taken into BR stock until 24 March 1993, when it was allocated to the Construction subsector at Immingham, being the last of the class to be accepted by BR. It was given the name *Bow Fell*, which it still carried when seen passing Micklefield at the head of train 6D71, the 12.05 Leeds–Lindsey empty tanks, on 2 May 1998. *Gavin Morrison*

Right:
No **60 016** entered BR service on 9 February 1993, allocated to the Construction subsector and based at Stewarts Lane. It was originally named *Langdale Pikes*, but these plates were removed in July 1997; it was renamed *Rail Magazine* at Cardiff Canton depot on 10 April 2000. In immaculate condition, it is seen here heading a Mountsorrel–Tyne stone train past Hasland on 23 May 2001. Behind the trees was once an LMS steam shed, which closed in 1964. *Gavin Morrison*

Above:
Completed on 2 March 1990 and accepted into BR stock on 30 October of that year, allocated to the Metals subsector at Thornaby, No **60 017** was originally named *Arenig Fawr*. On 8 November 1996 it was renamed *Shotton Works Centenary Year 1996* at Shotton Works. The locomotive was involved in an accident due to a landslip on the Settle & Carlisle line near Crosby Garrett Tunnel on 15 January 1999, when it ran into Class 156 'Super Sprinter' No 156 489. This picture, taken from the road bridge to the north of Derby station, shows the locomotive heading a train of iron slabs from Lackenby to Llanwern on 1 June 2002. *Gavin Morrison*

Left:
Having emerged from the Falcon Works in March 1990, No **60 018** *Moel Siabod* was allocated to the Construction subsector when it entered BR stock on 30 October 1990. However, the plates were removed during 1997, and the locomotive is currently unnamed. This photograph, taken on 8 October 2001, shows it approaching Wakefield Kirkgate and crossing over onto the lines for Pontefract with train 6E06, the 10.00 Bredbury–Roxby 'Binliner'. *Gavin Morrison*

Above:
Named *Wild Boar Fell* when completed in March 1990, No **60 019** joined the Construction subsector at Immingham in December 1990. It lost its name in May 1996 and ran for some time in Railfreight grey livery without decals before eventually being painted in EWS colours. It is seen approaching Grindleford on the heavy 6M85 11.55 Tunstead–Ratcliffe stone train on 18 May 2004; later that month it would be renamed *Pathfinder Tours — 30 years of Railtouring, 1973-2003*, (carried originally by Class 56 No 56 038), but these plates have since been removed.
Gavin Morrison

Right:
Five months after being taken into BR stock with the Metals subsector at Thornaby, No **60 020** *Great Whernside*, running light-engine, heads east past Eaglescliffe on 24 June 1991. The name would be removed in November 1996.
Gavin Morrison

Above:
The 'Binliner' services between the Manchester area and Roxby provided regular work for the Class 60s for more than 10 years, and only recently have Class 66s made an appearance. No **60 021** *Pen-y-Ghent* (a name originally carried by 'Peak' No D8, later renumbered 44 008) was allocated to the Metals subsector at Thornaby when it entered BR service on 14 December 1991. On 23 May 2002, unmarked and running without any subsector decals), the locomotive is seen approaching the Wakefield road bridge at Horbury, just east of Healey Mills Yard, with train 6E06, the 10.00 Bredbury–Roxby. The locomotive has since been renamed *Star of the East*. *Gavin Morrison*

Left:
After EWS took over there was a short period before the decision was taken to paint the fleet in the livery of the then parent company, Wisconsin Central, and following overhaul a number of the company's locomotives re-entered traffic in undercoat. Among these was a Class 60, No **60 022**, which until March 1996 had carried the name *Ingleborough* (another once carried by a 'Peak', in this case No D7, later 44 007). It is seen in undercoat passing Hunslet, Leeds, with the 13.32 empty gypsum containers from Newbiggin to Milford on 12 July 1996.
Gavin Morrison

Right:
When new No **60 023** joined the Metals subsector at Thornaby and was named *The Cheviot*, the plates being retained until March 1997. It is recorded as being the first member of the class to be accepted by BR, on 11 September 1990. On what can hardly be described as suitable work for a Class 60, the Warrington Arpley–St Helens tanks (6Z31), it approaches Winwick Junction, just north of Warrington, on 19 December 2002.
Gavin Morrison

Centre right:
Another locomotive allocated to the Metals subsector upon entering BR service on 17 December 1990 at Thornaby, No **60 024** lost its *Elizabeth Fry* name in March 1997 and has remained nameless since. The picture shows it approaching Twyford, on the Great Western main line, with a down stone train on 2 July 1999.
Gavin Morrison

Below:
One of the five members of the class to receive Loadhaul livery, No **60 025**, new as *Joseph Lister* but by now nameless, passes a popular photographic location at Caister Road, Barnetby, with a tank train for Immingham on 17 July 1996.
Gavin Morrison

Above:
Allocated to the Petroleum subsector, No **60 026** entered BR stock on 12 December 1990 as *William Caxton*. Still with Petroleum decals, it is heading along the East Coast main line just south of Colton Junction, near York, with train 6D43, the 14.16 Jarrow–Lindsey empty tanks, on 16 July 1994. The nameplates would be removed in September 1996. *Gavin Morrison*

Below:
Ever since they were introduced the Class 60s have worked the limestone trains from Swinden Quarry, on the old Grassington branch, to Dairycoates, Hull. Here No **60 027**, in original condition with Petroleum decals and *Joseph Banks* nameplates (since removed), snakes down the valley towards Skipton, where it will reverse, *en route* to Hull on 4 May 1995. *Gavin Morrison*

Right:
No **60 028** has lost its Metals subsector decals, which it had received when it entered BR service on 9 November 1990, but it still retains the name *John Flamsteed* as it heads north along the Erewash Valley line near Trowell with a train of empty bogie tanks on 15 February 2003. *Gavin Morrison*

Below:
Originally the Port Talbot–Llanwern ore trains were worked by triple-headed Class 37s; these were replaced by double-headed Class 56s, which in turn were replaced by a single Class 60. No **60 029** *Ben Nevis* was accepted into traffic with the Metals subsector at Thornaby on 26 November 1990 and is seen here passing Cardiff Canton depot, returning empty ore wagons to Port Talbot on 23 March 1993. On 4 July 1998 it would be renamed *Clitheroe Castle* in a ceremony held at Castle Cement's Clitheroe works. *Gavin Morrison*

Above:
A flash of sun on a dull, wet day catches No **60 030** being loaded at the Hunterston ore terminal on the Ayrshire coast before departing for the Ravenscraig steelworks near Motherwell on 13 June 1991. The locomotive was named *Cir Mhor* when it entered service with the Metals subsector on 21 November 1990, but the name was removed in June 1997. *Gavin Morrison*

Left:
After 3 miles and 64 yards of darkness train 6M05, the 09.30 Roxby–Northenden 'Binliner', emerges into the sunlight at the west end of Standedge North Tunnel and passes the site of the closed Diggle station on 16 December 2005. The tunnel was built between 1890 and 1894; the now disused single-bore tunnels are to the right of the picture. No **60 031** was named *Ben Lui* when it entered service with the Metals subsector on 2 May 1991, but the name was removed during December 1997 and replaced by *ABP Connect* in a ceremony held at the Hams Hall terminal on 21 June 2002. Class 158 No 158 761 is on a Manchester Piccadilly–Hull service. *Gavin Morrison*

Above:
Clay Cross Junction, a few miles south of Chesterfield, is the point where the Erewash Valley route to Nottingham and Toton splits from the line to Derby. On 21 August 2004 No **60 032** heads an empty Llanwern–Lackenby train. By now in Transrail livery, the locomotive still carries the name *William Booth*, which it received at Nottingham station on 23 November 1990, although it did not enter service, with the Petroleum subsector, until 3 December. *Gavin Morrison*

Right:
On 4 September 1997, two months after receiving the superb British Steel blue livery, No **60 033** is still in immaculate external condition as it heads east just past Cross Gates station, near Leeds, with an empty Hunslet–Lindsey tank train. It was originally named *Anthony Ashley Cooper* when it was accepted by BR on 22 February 1991 into the Petroleum subsector, but the name was removed in June 1997; the following month it became *Tees Steel Express*. *Gavin Morrison*

Left:
No **60 034** makes slow progress as it toils up the gradient towards the Ebbw Vale steelworks complex with a heavy steel train on 20 June 1993. After the closure of the works the line closed, but is to be reinstated for passenger services. The locomotive entered BR service with the Metals subsector on 12 December 1990 named *Carnedd Llewelyn*, a name it still carries. *Gavin Morrison*

Below:
When accepted by BR on 23 April 1991 No **60 035** was named *Florence Nightingale* and allocated to the Construction subsector; it was to have been named *Snowdon*, but this was already in use on a Class 86 electric. It is seen here heading a Port Talbot–Llanwern ore train across the River Usk at Newport on 22 March 1993. The plates would be removed at Toton in October 2001. *Gavin Morrison*

Right:
Entering traffic with the Metals subsector on 25 June 1991, No **60 036** was originally named *Squrr Na Ciche*. This was removed in September 1997, and on 15 July 1999 the locomotive was given the new name of *GEFCO*. Here it catches the weak winter sunlight as it enters Healey Mills Yard from the east for a crew change while hauling train 6M05, the 09.40 Roxby–Northenden 'Binliner', on 15 December 2005. On the right can be seen Class 47 No 47 811 on the approach to the wagon-repair works, where it had suffered a minor derailment. *Gavin Morrison*

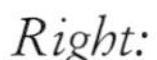

Right:
No **60 037** was the first of the class to work a Lackenby–Corby steel train, being seen passing Burton Salmon on 8 April 1991, only four days after it had entered traffic with the Metals subsector. At this time it was named *Helvellyn*, this name having been chosen in preference to the original suggestion of *Blencathra*; it would be removed in April 1997 and replaced in May of that year by *Aberddawan / Aberthaw* at the power station of the same name. *Gavin Morrison*

Left:
Apart from the limestone dust on the cab roof No **60 038** looks very smart in its Loadhaul livery on 1 May 2001 as it heads train 6E06, the 09.40 Bredbury–Roxby 'Binliner', just to the east of Huddersfield on the approach to Bradley Junction. The locomotive had entered traffic on 4 March 1991 with the Metals subsector, with the name *Bidean Nam Bian*, but the plates were removed in May 1995. It remained nameless until 19 March 2002, when, in a ceremony held at Immingham Nordic Terminal, it became *AvestaPolarit*.
Gavin Morrison

Above:
The Class 60s took over from the double-headed Class 37s on the Scunthorpe–Immingham ore trains in the early 1990s and have remained on these duties since. No **60 039** entered BR stock on 9 May 1991, named *Glastonbury Tor* and allocated to the Petroleum subsector. Now nameless and in EWS livery, it heads a loaded train westwards past New Barnetby on 25 March 2003. *Gavin Morrison*

Left:
Taken into stock on 6 February 1992, No **60 040** was allocated to the Construction subsector and until July 1996 carried the name *Brecon Beacons*. It is seen passing Kensington Olympia station with train 7O02, the 12.33 Acton Yard–Woking hoppers, on 23 February 1995. *Jason Rogers*

Right:
Allocated to the Construction subsector when it entered BR service on 20 June 1991, No **60 041** originally carried the name *High Willhays*, which it lost during October 1996. Here, nameless and in EWS livery, the locomotive passes through Stainforth station with an empty steel train from Scunthorpe to Lackenby on 19 May 1998. The skyline is dominated by Hatfield Colliery, which had recently closed but is about to be reopened. *Gavin Morrison*

Below:
In Railfreight triple-grey livery but with Mainline decals, No **60 042** *Dunkery Beacon* crosses Holes Bay and heads towards Poole on 30 November 1996 with train 6V13, the Furzebrook–Hallen Marsh LPG tanks, which traffic has since been lost to the railways. New to the Construction subsector on 29 May 1991, the locomotive would have its original nameplates removed during February 1997, to be renamed in July 1999 as *The Hundered of Hoo*. *Gavin Morrison*

Left:
Allocated to the Construction subsector when it entered BR service on 26 June 1991, No **60 043** originally carried the name *Yes Tor*, which it lost in February 1997. Now nameless, it is seen climbing away from Wakefield past Walton with train 6E06, the 10.00 Bredbury–Roxby 'Binliner', on 16 July 1998. On the left of the picture is the now virtually unused spur from the old Midland main line. *Gavin Morrison*

Below:
In the attractive blue livery of Mainline but now with large EWS sticker on the side, No **60 044** shunts stone wagons at Peak Forest after working a train from Washwood Heath on 9 June 2006. It has lost the *Ailsa Craig* nameplates which it carried when new in 1990. *Gavin Morrison*

Above:
The location of Hagg Lane crossing, at the east end of Gascoigne Wood Colliery (now closed), shows to advantage the length of the Dairycoates–Swinden Quarry train. On 19 November 2004 No **60 045** was in charge, carrying the name *Permanent Way Institution*, which it received on 8 November 1997. Originally named *Josephine Butler*, the locomotive had entered traffic with the Construction subsector on 25 March 1991. *Gavin Morrison*

Below:
In 2006 EWS decided that those members of the class that had not received the maroon EWS livery should have large yellow EWS stickers applied over the previous decals. Thus adorned, No **60 046** is seen here passing Mirfield with train 6M22, the 12.40 Hunslet–Tunstead cement, on 10 April 2006. Allocated to the Construction subsector when it entered service on 4 April 1991, it still carries its original name, *William Wilberforce*. Considering that it was 15 years old when the picture was taken, the paintwork still looks reasonably smart. *Gavin Morrison*

Left:
In connection with an Old Oak Common open day on 18 August 1991 several 'Greenford Grinder' specials ran from Paddington around the Greenford loop. They were 'topped-and-tailed' by Foster Yeoman Class 59 No 59 005 *Kenneth J. Painter* and Class 60 No **60 047** *Robert Owen,* the latter, photographed from the A4 road bridge, being seen heading one of the specials past Acton *Gavin Morrison*

Below:
No **60 048** entered service with the Coal subsector on 30 April 1991 with the name *Saddleback*. However, in August 1997 these plates were removed, and in a ceremony held later that month at Clydeport, Hunterston, the locomotive was renamed *Eastern*. By now in EWS livery, the locomotive is seen awaiting its next duty alongside No 60 022 at Peak Forest on 9 June 2006. *Gavin Morrison*

Above:
Wrawby Junction, just to the east of Barnetby, has long been a favourite location for photographers and retains some of the finest signal gantries surviving on the network. Returning to Scunthorpe on 26 January 2001 with a train of empty iron-ore hoppers from Frodingham, No **60 049** *Scafell* still carried its Petroleum subsector decals, which it received when accepted into service on 7 May 1991. *Gavin Morrison*

Centre right:
No **60 050** entered service on 8 March 1991 with the Metals subsector and carrying the name *Roseberry Topping*. In this picture it is heading an ore train from Hunterston to Ravenscraig at Whifflet Junction, not far from Motherwell, on 14 June 1991. The name would be removed in November 1990. *Gavin Morrison*

Right:
Neatly framed by the electrification masts on the goods line to the south of Doncaster station, No **60 051**, in EWS livery, heads towards the yards at the south of the town on 7 May 2002. It had entered service with the Petroleum subsector on 10 April 1991 as *Mary Somerville*, a name it lost in April 1997. *Gavin Morrison*

Left:
Having entered traffic just five weeks previously, on 9 May, No **60 052** *Goat Fell*, complete with Metals subsector decals, heads east through Kilwinning station on 13 June 1991 with an MGR working from Hunterston. Its original nameplates were would be removed during May 1997, to be replaced on 25 August 1998 by the lengthy name *Glofa Twr / Tower Colliery — The Last Deep Mine in Wales.*
Gavin Morrison

Above:
Having entered service on 25 April 1991 with the Petroleum subsector, No **60 053** *John Reith* was engaged on Metals work on 4 April 1996, when it was photographed hauling a train of empty steel flats, just to the east of Scunthorpe station. On the right of the picture is a very clean Loadhaul-liveried Class 37/5, No 37 698, on MGR duties. During February 1997 No 60 053 would lose its original name in favour of *Nordic Terminal*.
Gavin Morrison

Above:
The Furzebrook–Hallen Marsh LPG tanks are shown arriving at their destination on 19 June 1993 behind No **60 054** *Charles Babbage*, which had entered traffic with the Petroleum subsector on 3 May 1991. At the time of writing this locomotive was last of the class to retain Petroleum decals. *Gavin Morrison*

Below:
Fiddler's Ferry power station dominates the skyline as No **60 055**, in Transrail livery, returns some former National Power coal wagons to the yards at Warrington on 9 November 2001. Named *Thomas Barnardo* since entering service with the Coal subsector on 6 June 1991, the locomotive is pictured heading east towards the level crossing at Warrington Monks sidings. *Gavin Morrison*

Left:
Still bearing the name *William Beveridge*, which it received upon entering traffic with the Petroleum subsector on 24 May 1991, No **60 056** passes beneath the listed Bennerley Viaduct, which used to carry the former Great Northern line between Derby and Nottingham, on 22 March 2003. The train is a diverted Lackenby–Llanwern service, travelling via the Erewash Valley line. Despite being still in original livery with the addition of Transrail decals, the locomotive would appear to have been cleaned for some special occasion. *Gavin Morrison*

Left:
Still carrying Coal decals 11 years after it entered service with the subsector (on 1 June 1991), No **60 057** *Adam Smith* is seen heading train 6E06, the 09.40 Bredbury–Roxby 'Binliner', past Belle Vue, Wakefield, on 26 September 2002. It is hard to believe that the old Lancashire & Yorkshire steam shed used to stand on the right of the picture. *Gavin Morrison*

Left:
Displaying the Coal subsector decals applied when it entered service on 7 July 1991, No **60 058** *John Howard* enters the siding to the waste-recycling plant at Pendleton, near Manchester, on 27 July 1992. The locomotive was to have its nameplates removed during 2003, while the cooling towers of Agecroft power station, visible here in the background, were demolished several years ago. *Gavin Morrison*

Right:
No **60 059** entered service with the Metals subsector on 5 July 1991, named *Samuel Plimsoll*, but the plates were removed in April 1995, when it was sent to Brush for repair, having been selected as the first of the class to be repainted in Loadhaul livery. Freshly repainted and with masking still in place, it is seen outside the firm's Loughborough works on 3 May alongside newly built Class 92 electric No 92015. The '60' would be renamed *Swinden Dalesman* on 20 June 1995 at Hillhead Quarry, having been transported by road from Hindlow for a three-day trade exhibition. *Gavin Morrison*

Above:
Until 2006 No **60 060** *James Watt* continued to display the Coal subsector decals applied when it entered traffic on 28 June 1991, but subsequently EWS stickers have been applied. It is seen here at Buxworth heading train 6H55, the 09.15 Bletchley–Peak Forest RMC hoppers, on 9 September 2004. *Gavin Morrison*

Above:
Accepted into stock by BR on 6 June 1991, No **60 061** was originally allocated to the Coal subsector and carried the name *Alexander Graham Bell*, but by the date of this picture, 9 September 2004, it had gained Transrail decals and lost its nameplates. It is seen approaching Cowburn Tunnel from the west with train 6M85, the 12.05 from Tunstead to Ratcliffe power station. *Gavin Morrison*

Left:
Train 6D04, the 11.18 limestone empties from Hull Dairycoates to Rylston, heads through the new Leeds City station on 2 May 2000. At this time No **60 062** retained its *Samuel Johnson* nameplates (since removed), but Transrail decals had replaced those of the Petroleum subsector, with which it had entered traffic on 17 June 1991.
Gavin Morrison

Right:
No **60 063** *James Murray* was allocated to the Petroleum subsector when it entered service on 13 June 1991 but had gained Transrail decals by 23 September 2003, when it was photographed at New Mills Junction heading train 6H55, the 09.15 Bletchley–Peak Forest RMC hoppers. *Gavin Morrison*

Below:
No **60 064** was one of three members of the class to have Loadhaul decals applied to its original Railfreight grey livery. Still carrying the name *Back Tor*, with which it entered service with the Petroleum subsector on 28 August 1991, it is shown passing Ordsall Lane, Salford, at the head of a lengthy engineering train on 23 January 2005.
Gavin Morrison

Left:
The hawthorn bushes are in full bloom at Brumber Bridge, near Colton Junction, south of York, on 22 May 2004 as a Tilcon train from the North East heads back to Swinden Quarry, headed by EWS-liveried No **60 065**. Named *Kinder Low* when it entered service on 17 September 1991 with the Petroleum subsector, it had these plates removed in August 1999 and was renamed *Spirit of Jaguar* in a ceremony held at Castle Bromwich on 18 March 2003. *Gavin Morrison*

Below:
In original condition, with the Coal subsector decals with which it entered traffic on 22 August 1991, No **60 066** *John Logie Baird* passes Diggle at the head of 6M06, the 09.40 Roxby–Bredbury 'Binliner' on 11 October 1994. To the right of the train was once a busy marshalling yard, while in the background (right) can just be seen the entrance to Standedge Tunnel. *Gavin Morrison*

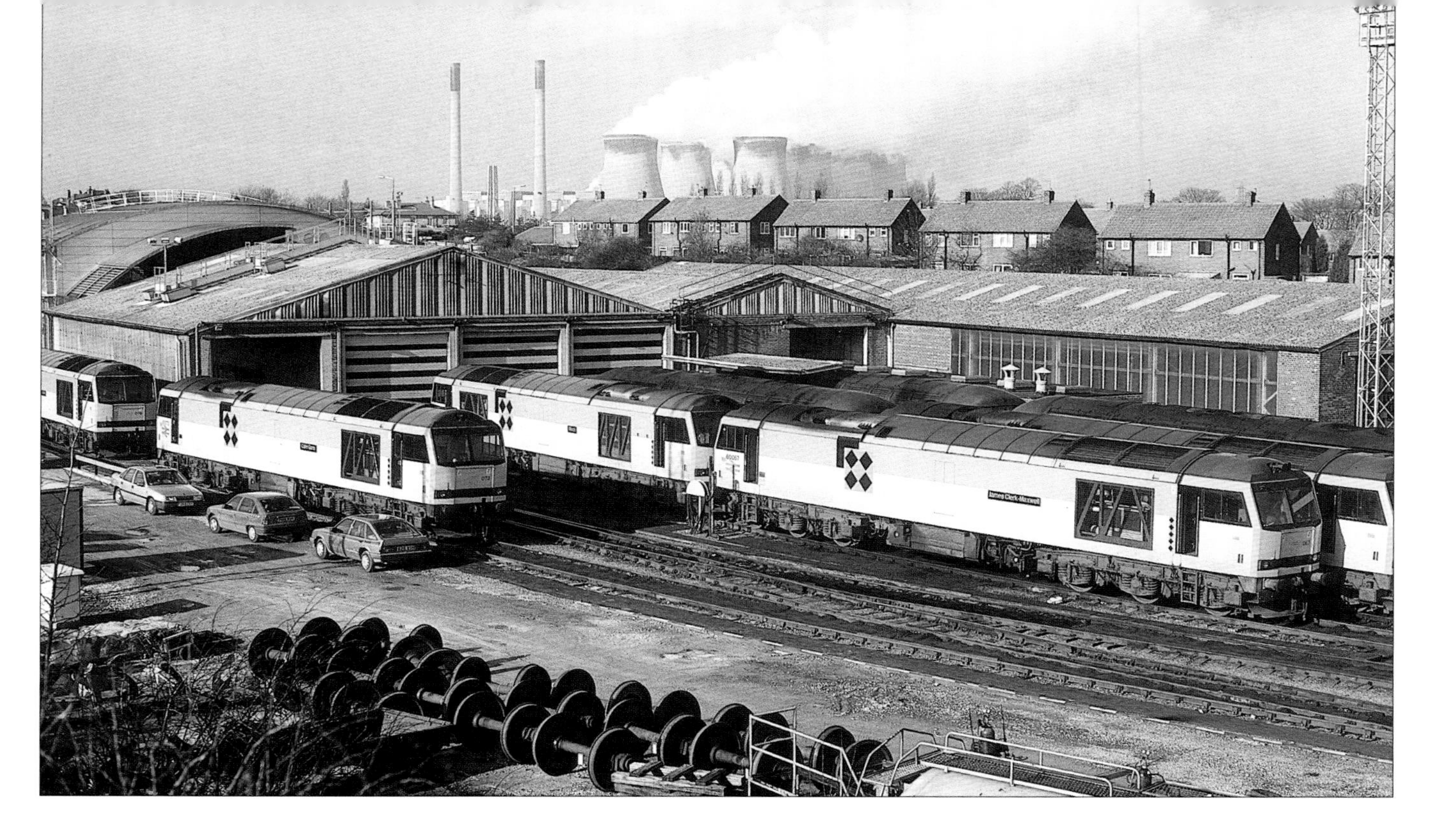

Above:
No **60 067** *James Clerk-Maxwell*, which entered service on 20 September 1991, is prominent amongst a clutch of five Coal-subsector Class 60s on shed at Knottingley depot on 8 February 1994. This was a common sight in the early 1990s, but activity at this location is nowadays much reduced following the closure of the Gascoigne Wood pit. *Gavin Morrison*

Above:
Although retaining the *Charles Darwin* nameplates which it carried upon entering service on 16 October 1991, No **60 068** had lost its Coal subsector decals by 25 March 2002, when it was photographed at Camp Hill, Birmingham, on a light southbound working. *Gavin Morrison*

Left:
On 1 September 1991 newly delivered No **60 069** *Humphry Davy* appeared at the Worksop open day, which featured workings along the South Yorkshire Joint line. With Coal subsector decals already applied, it is seen passing Dinnington with one of the many passenger workings. Despite its participation in this event the locomotive would not formally be taken into stock until the following day. *Gavin Morrison*

Below left:
Having entered service with the Coal subsector on 28 October 1991, No **60 070** *John Loudon McAdam* is seen stabled in the siding on the north side of Skipton station on 2 September 1995, awaiting its next duty from Swinden Quarry. On the right is Class 47/7 No 47 721 *Saint Bede*, waiting to head north with the 'Royal Scotsman' once its passengers have returned from visiting the town, while in the station is a Class 144 diesel unit. *Gavin Morrison*

Above right:
In the livery of the Coal subsector, with which it had entered traffic on 19 September 1991, No **60 071** *Dorothy Garrod* approaches Pinxton on 13 November 1992 with a rake of what appear to be mainly new MGR wagons. Seen about to pass under the M1 motorway, the train is on the Worksop–Shirebrook line, which carries on to join the Erewash Valley main line at Pye Bridge Junction. This is also the point at which the line to the Bentinck Colliery (now closed) branched off. *Gavin Morrison*

Right:
New to the Coal subsector on 21 October 1991, No **60 072** *Cairn Toul* is seen hauling loaded MGR wagons through the discharge point at Ratcliffe power station on a glorious 2 October 1995. *Paul Corrie*

072

Left:
Entering traffic on 22 November 1991, No **60 073** *Cairn Gorm* was originally allocated to the Coal subsector, but by the time this photograph was taken, on 25 June 2003, the 'black diamonds' decal had been replaced by the Mainline logo. The locomotive is seen in charge of train 6M06, the empty 17.13 'Binliner' from Roxby to Bredbury, passing Templeborough on the 'back route' into Sheffield from Rotherham. *Gavin Morrison*

Below:
New to the Coal subsector on 25 November 1991, an immaculate No **60 074** *Braeriach* opens up as it passes Dinnington on the South Yorkshire Joint line with a loaded MGR train heading towards Worksop on 31 May 1996. *Gavin Morrison*

Right:
Pictured just to the east of Mirfield station at the head of train 6E06, the 10.00 Bredbury–Roxby 'Binliner', No **60 075** recovers from a signal check as it heads for the bi-directional section to Thornhill Junction on its journey east on 13 July 2006. Originally named *Liathach*, the locomotive had entered traffic on 4 December 1991 with the Coal subsector.
Gavin Morrison

Below:
Hauling one of the regular ballast workings from Penmaenmawr Quarry, on the North Wales coast, No **60 076** is seen at the head of train 6P22, the 11.00 from the quarry sidings to Basford Hall, Crewe, on 27 June 2000. Still in grey livery, the locomotive displays the Mainline logo that replaced the Coal subsector decals with which it entered service on 22 November 1991. It lost its original *Suilven* nameplates in January 1997.
Jason Rogers

Above:
Allocated to the Coal subsector upon entering traffic on 23 November 1991, No **60 077** *Canisp* had gained Mainline logos by July 1996, when it was photographed climbing out of Bristol and passing Narroways Hill Junction on Ashley Down Bank with the impressive 6V13 Furzebrook–Hallen Marsh LPG tanks. Sadly this train no longer runs. *J. Turner*

Left:
In the attractive Mainline blue livery, No **60 078** snakes across the crossovers at Monk Fryston on 6 February 2001, heading the diverted 6D04 11.18 Hull Dairycoates–Rylston train, which at this point is travelling south on its journey north. The diversion, via Burton Salmon and Castleford, was due to the rebuilding of Leeds City station. Originally allocated to the Petroleum subsector, the locomotive had entered service on 26 November 1991 named *Stac Pollaidh*, but the plates were removed in January 1996. *Gavin Morrison*

Right:
The now closed Brocklesby station is the location for this picture of No **60 079**, in grey with Mainline logos, heading a loaded coal train from Immingham Docks on 16 June 2003. It was allocated to the Petroleum subsector when it entered service on 17 January 1992, named *Foinaven*. One nameplate was missing by January 1996, and the other was removed during March 1997. *Gavin Morrison*

Below:
No **60 080**, named *Kinder Scout* and belonging to the Construction subsector, to which it was allocated upon entering traffic on 23 November 1991, heads train 6M05, the 09.30 Roxby–Northenden 'Binliner', past Bradley Junction, to the east of Huddersfield, on 25 February 1994. By this time the spur linking the ex-LNWR main line with the ex-Lancashire & Yorkshire main line was out of use, but this has recently been reinstated, allowing through services to be operated again every hour between Huddersfield and Bradford via Halifax. *Gavin Morrison*

Above:
Despite retaining the livery of the Construction subsector, with which it had entered traffic on 3 December 1991, No **60 081** *Bleaklow Hill* leaves the steelworks at Port Talbot with an ore train for Llanwern on 22 June 1993. Later in its career this locomotive would be outshopped in lined Great Western green livery with brass cabside numbers, to be renamed *Isambard Kingdom Brunel* at an open day held at Old Oak Common on 5 August 2000. *Gavin Morrison*

Below:
No **60 082** entered traffic with the Petroleum subsector on 3 December 1991 as *Mam Tor*, although the original intension had been to name it *Pen-y-Fan*. Temporarily renamed *Hillhead '93* for an exhibition at that quarry on 14 June 1993, it later had its *Mam Tor* restored. Here we see the locomotive, still in grey but with Transrail logos, descending from Copy Pit towards Portsmouth with the empty Preston Docks–Lindsey tanks on 12 September 2005. *Gavin Morrison*

Right:
No **60 083** entered service on 27 March 1992 with the Construction subsector named *Shining Tor*, but these plates were removed during February 1997, and on 30 August 1998 the locomotive was renamed *Mountsorrel*. By now in EWS livery, it is seen passing the site of the marshalling yards to the east of Brighouse with a rail train from Castleton to Toton on 22 April 2004. *Gavin Morrison*

Above:
After spending nearly 14 months in the yard at the Falcon Works No **60 084** *Cross Fell* entered traffic on 11 January 1993 with the Construction subsector. On the weekend of 22/23 May 1993 it was used on a tour around the North West of England, organised by Pathfinder Tours, using a wide variety of motive power that also included examples of Classes 20, 26, 31, 37, 56 and 58s. It is seen on the Saturday, heading west across Accrington Viaduct after visiting the Padiham branch, with Class 26s Nos 26 003 and 26 005 just visible at the rear of the train. *Gavin Morrison*

Left:
In the livery of the Construction subsector, to which it was allocated upon entering traffic on 13 December 1991, No **60 085** *Axe Edge* passes through Bolton in the evening light of 26 May 1992 with a train from the Metal Box Company's sidings at Westhoughton. On 6 November 2000 this locomotive would be involved in a serious accident at Llanwern yard, being hit by an errant No 60 025. Out of traffic for around 11 months, it would return to be renamed Mini — Pride of Oxford in a ceremony at BMW's 'Oxford Facility' (otherwise known as Cowley) on 21 November 2001. *Gavin Morrison*

Below:
The hawthorn blossom is past its best at Dudfleet Lane, Horbury, near Wakefield, as No **60 086** *Schiehallion*, still in grey livery with the addition of Mainline logos, heads east with train 6E06, the 09.40 Bredbury–Roxby 'Binliner', on 30 May 2003. New to traffic on 16 January 1992, the locomotive was originally allocated to the Construction subsector. *Gavin Morrison*

Right:
Another view featuring train 6E06, this time on 10 February 2000, headed by No **60 087**. At this date the locomotive still retained the *Slioch* nameplates with which it had entered traffic on 18 December 1991 but had had its original Coal subsector decals replaced by those of Mainline. The photograph was taken from the overbridge at Addingford Lane, Horbury, before the line enters a deep cutting that was once a tunnel. In the background can be seen the lights of Healey Mills Yard. *Gavin Morrison*

Above:
On 10 April 1997, in the days before the 6E17 Peak Forest–Leeds Stourton working was routed via Standedge and Batley, No **60 088** *Buachaille Etive Mor* passes Wortley Junction South at Copley Hill, Leeds, having travelled via the Hope Valley, Sheffield and Wakefield Westgate. Originally allocated to the Coal subsector, the locomotive entered traffic on 20 January 1992 with the incorrect spelling of '*More*' on the nameplates; these were replaced in June of that year with newly cast plates. *Gavin Morrison*

Above:
Having begun its career in the Petroleum subsector on 8 January 1992, No **60 089** *Arcuil* had these plates removed early in 2002 and on 8 June was renamed *The Railway Horse* in a ceremony at the Severn Valley Railway. It is seen on 29 August 2004 heading a train of empty ex-National Power coal wagons past a builder's yard at Lea Green on its way back to Liverpool Docks from Fiddler's Ferry power station. *Gavin Morrison*

Below:
Heading No 60 013 *Robert Boyle*, which had failed somewhere in the Liverpool area, No **60 090** *Quinag* passes Winwick, near Warrington, with a train of ex-National Power wagons *en route* from Liverpool Docks to Fiddler's Ferry power station on 5 July 2004. Note that at this time it retained the Coal subsector decals with which it had entered traffic on 3 February 1992. *Gavin Morrison*

Above:
Another member of the class to retain its Coal subsector decals until at least the end of 2005 was No **60 091**, named *An Teallach* when it was accepted by BR on 3 February 1992. Here it is approaching Brocklesby station with a train of empty ore wagons returning to Immingham from Scunthorpe on 16 June 2003. *Gavin Morrison*

Below:
Originally to have been named *Boar of Badenoch* (subsequently applied to no 60 100), No **60 092** entered traffic nameless with the Coal subsector on 31 January 1992, eventually named *Reginald Munns* at Worksop on 21 September. Here it is passing the Port Talbot steelworks with the heavily loaded Robeston–Theale tanks on 22 June 1993. *Gavin Morrison*

Above:
Another Class 60 to enter traffic unnamed was No **60 093**, which began its career with the Coal subsector on 21 February 1992 and was eventually named *Jack Stirk* on 21 September. The name was replaced on 20 July 2004 by *Adrian Harrington 1955-2003 Royal Navy / Burges Salmon*, but these plates in turn were later removed, and by the date of this photograph — 1 March 2006 — the locomotive was again nameless. It is seen approaching Normanton station with train 6M17, the 10.18 Leeds Stourton–Peak Forest empty stone working; the tail of the train has just passed Altofts Junction. On the right of the picture is the site of the old Midland Railway shed, which turned out to be the last active steam shed east of the Pennines in Yorkshire. *Gavin Morrison*

Left:
Allocated to the Construction subsector when it entered traffic on 20 February 1992, No **60 094** *Tryfan* heads along the Hope Valley just east of Edale station on 27 January 2004 with train 6M85, the 11.55 Tunstead–Ratcliffe working. It has since been repainted in EWS livery and renamed *Rugby Flyer*.
Gavin Morrison

Above:
The loaded stone train from Swinden Quarry, on the old Grassington branch, passes Guiseley Junction, Shipley, on its way to Hull behind No **60 095** *Crib Goch* of the Construction subsector. The photograph was taken on 30 July 1992, at which time the locomotive had been in service for only four months. It would lose its nameplates in July 1997. *Gavin Morrison*

Below:
No **60 096** entered service on 13 May 1992 with the Construction subsector as *Ben Macdui*, a name it was to retain until 2002. By now in EWS livery, the locomotive is shown approaching the closed Gascoigne Wood pit in the Selby Coalfield with train 6D04, the 11.18 empties from Hull Dairycoates to Rylston, on 31 October 2005. *Gavin Morrison*

Left:
Another photograph featuring the limestone train from Swinden Quarry to Hull, this time approaching Wortley Junction, Leeds, on 25 March 1993. No **60 097** *Pillar* was another locomotive allocated from new to the Construction subsector and at the time of this photograph had been in service for only four months. It has since been renamed *ABP Port of Grimsby & Immingham*, while Wortley Junction is now disfigured by electrification masts for local trains on the Aire Valley line. *Gavin Morrison*

Below:
The 1,000th locomotive built at the Brush Falcon Works since 1945, No **60 098** carried a plaque to this effect and upon entering service — with the Construction subsector — on 22 December 1992 was given the name *Charles Francis Brush*. It is seen in EWS colours passing Colton Junction, south of York, with train 6D43, the 14.16 Jarrow–Lindsey empty tanks, on 8 May 2003; later that year it would be one of the first of the class to be placed in store, from which at the time of writing it has not been reinstated. *Gavin Morrison*

Right:
No **60 099** began its career, with the Construction subsector, on 18 December 1992 but did not receive its name — *Ben More Assynt* — until 18 March 1993. By now adorned with Mainline logos, the locomotive approaches Burton-upon-Trent station with train 6M57, the 08.31 Lindsey–Kingsbury tanks, on 6 April 2002. *Gavin Morrison*

Above:
When it entered service on 9 December 1992 with the Construction subsector No **60 100** was named *Boar of Badenoch*, although the plates had apparently been attached nearly nine months previously. They were removed in January 2003, and on 28 June of that year the locomotive was renamed *Pride of Acton*. In EWS livery, it is seen passing Crowle *en route* to Scunthorpe on 20 April 2004. *Gavin Morrison*

Passenger Workings

Left:
Although the type has always been in demand for railtours, instances of Class 60s working scheduled passenger trains have been rare. On Saturday 11 August 1991 special trains, employing a wide variety of motive power, were run along the North Wales Coast main line between Crewe and Llandudno to raise funds for charity. One such was double-headed by Nos 60 044 *Ailsa Craig*, with Metals subsector decals and 60 061 *Alexander Graham Bell*, seen passing Holywell running rather late — and very fast for Class 60s. *Gavin Morrison*

Above:
The special of 11 August 1991 on the outward leg to Llandudno, approaching Llandudno Junction from the east with No 60 061 *Alexander Graham Bell* leading No 60 044 *Ailsa Craig*. *Gavin Morrison*

Above:
As described on page 4, on 24 April 1993 No 60 094 *Tryfan* was unexpectedly diagrammed to work the 1M02 09.24 Edinburgh–Birmingham service — diverted due to engineering work on the West Coast main line — over the Settle–Carlisle route. The train was photographed by a surprised author (no mobile phones in those days!) as it headed south across Whalley Viaduct. *Gavin Morrison*

Right:
Another double-headed combination appeared on this Pathfinder special of 17 September 1994, No 60 085 *Axe Edge* of the Construction subsector piloting Petroleum's No 60 082 *Mam Tor*. The train is seen approaching Ditton from Warrington, with Fiddler's Ferry power station in the background. *Gavin Morrison*

Above:
Over the weekend of 25/26 April 1992 Pathfinder Tours, in conjunction with Regional Railways, organised a series of special workings around the North West of England, using a wide variety of motive power. Having arrived behind Class 20s Nos 20 154 and 20 057 (just visible in the background), the 13.28 from Manchester departs Morecambe on the Sunday behind No 60 046 *William Wilberforce*. *Gavin Morrison*

Left:
The weekend of 25/26 April 1992 also saw No 60 056 *William Beveridge*, with Coal subsector decals, piloting Class 37/4 No 37 419 on a Blackpool–Manchester Victoria working, seen leaving Bolton on the Saturday. *Gavin Morrison*

Right:
Another special working run as part of the Pathfinder/Regional Railways weekend saw No 60 095 *Crib Goch* passing Agecroft with the 14.48 Manchester–Barrow on Saturday 25 April 1992.
Gavin Morrison

Below:
Another Pathfinder/Regional Railways special during the weekend of 25/26 April 1992 saw No 60 095 *Crib Goch* diagrammed for Saturday's 10.17 Manchester–Southport service, seen arriving at Southport. The return working, the 11.35 to Manchester, was hauled by Class 58 No 58 009. *Gavin Morrison*

Left:
Another joint venture between Pathfinder Tours and Regional Railways, on 22 May 1993, saw a Class 60 visit Heysham. Pictured leaving the resort is No 60 097 *Pillar*, with Class 56 No 56 098 at the rear of the train. The line to the left serves the nuclear power station. *Gavin Morrison*

Centre left:
On Saturdays during December 1991 special motive power was organised by Regional Railways for the morning Leeds–Carlisle service train, which generated a large number of passengers. On the 28th No 60 022 *Ingleborough* piloted Class 31/4 No 31 418; seen passing Ais Gill *en route* for Carlisle, the train was running some 2hr 45min late owing to a points failure earlier in the day at Neville Hill.
Gavin Morrison

Below left:
As described on page 34, on 18 August 1991 an open day was held at Old Oak Common, and a special provided to take visitors on a circular tour around the Greenford loop from Paddington. At one end was No 60 047 *Robert Owen*, at the other Class 59/0 No 59 005 *Kenneth J. Painter*. The 'Greenford Grinder' is seen passing an HST just outside Paddington station. *Gavin Morrison*

Above right:
Another view of the 'Greenford Grinder', run in conjunction with the open day at Old Oak Common on 18 August 1991. Seen passing Park Royal, the train is headed by No 60 047 *Robert Owen*, with Class 59 No 59 005 *Kenneth J. Painter* bringing up the rear. *Gavin Morrison*

Right:
In conjunction with an open day held at Cambridge on 14 September 1991, Network SouthEast operated passenger services along the King's Lynn–Middleton Towers route. One of these was headed by No 60 048 *Saddleback*, seen approaching King's Lynn with two Class 312 EMU sets. *Gavin Morrison*

Greenford
Grinder
047

048

097
15
0

084

Left:
With No 56 098 at the rear, No 60 097 *Pillar* passes Morecambe Junction before heading down the branch to Heysham with the Pathfinder Tours / Regional Railways special of 22 May 1993. *Gavin Morrison*

Below left:
Returning from a visit to the Padiham branch on 23 May 1993, No 60 084 *Cross Fell* passes Rose Grove station westbound with a Pathfinder special. (Page 51 refers.) On the rear are Class 26s Nos 26 003 and 26 005, which had hauled the train back up the incline from Padiham to Rose Grove. *Gavin Morrison*

Above:
Having arrived behind Class 47/3 No 47 315, Pathfinder's 'Spinning Spectron' railtour of 19 June 1999 reversed at Goole, where Loadhaul-liveried No 60 025 *Joseph Lister* took over. The special is seen passing Holmes Bridge, Rotherham, on the return leg to Sheffield. *Gavin Morrison*

Centre left:
Adorned with an EWS sticker, No 60 028 *John Flamsteed* heads a Pathfinder special towards Immingham past the now closed Gascoigne Wood pit, in the Selby coalfield, on 30 September 2006. The pit has now been dismantled. *Gavin Morrison*

Below left:
Another Pathfinder special, headed by EWS-liveried No 60 038 *AvestaPolarit*, waits at Hexthorpe Bridge, Doncaster, for a Virgin 'Voyager' to pass on a southbound CrossCountry service on 16 September 2003. *Gavin Morrison*

Liveries

Railfreight

Left:
The line from Newport to the steelworks at Ebbw Vale climbed all the way up the valley. In 1993 most of the steel trains for the works ran at night, but three were scheduled on Sunday afternoons. On 20 June No 60 034 *Carnedd Llewelyn* makes slow progress passing Llanhilleth with a heavy train for the works. After the steelworks closed, so did the branch, but there are plans to reopen it for passenger services in the near future. *Gavin Morrison*

Below:
The line through Wensleydale used to link the Settle & Carlisle line with the East Coast main line at Northallerton. Through passenger services were withdrawn in 1954, and those between Hawes and Garsdale in 1958. However, the line remained open for stone traffic to Redmire Quarry and MoD traffic to Catterick Camp, the former ceasing in December 1992. On 16 December, during the last week of stone traffic operation, No 60 030 *Cir Mhor* passes the then closed station at Bedale (the signalbox being still in use for the level crossing) on its way to Redmire. After several 'last' specials the line was 'mothballed' but would eventually be reopened for MoD traffic and taken over by the Wensleydale Railway Co, which now operates a public passenger service as well as hosting occasional visiting specials. *Gavin Morrison*

Right:
Bound for Llanwern, No 60 029 *Ben Nevis* heads a loaded iron-ore train from Port Talbot past Miskin, on the Western Region main line between Swansea and Cardiff, on 21 June 1993. *Gavin Morrison*

Below:
A loaded steel train from Scunthorpe to Lackenby heads north along the East Coast main line on the Selby diversion at Rythir (Milepost 179) behind No 60 023 *The Cheviot* on 17 September 1996. *Gavin Morrison*

Construction subsector

Left:
No 60 081 *Bleaklow Hill* working a Port Talbot–Llanwern ore train, on 22 June 1993, photographed from the multi-storey car park at Bridgend. *Gavin Morrison*

Left:
Pictured just to the north of Skipton station, No 60 095 *Crib Goch* has run round the Swinden Quarry–Hull Dairycoates Tilcon limestone train before continuing its journey eastwards on 30 July 1992. *Gavin Morrison*

Left:
On 21 June 1993, long before it became the celebrity locomotive of the class (see pages 110 and 111), No 60 081 *Bleaklow Hill* is seen in the loop at Miskin, waiting for an HST to pass, at the head of the empties from Llanwern to Port Talbot. *Gavin Morrison*

Right:
Seen passing Aberbeeg, another of the Sunday-afternoon steel trains to Ebbw Vale (see page 68) makes its way up the valley behind No 60 081 *Bleaklow Hill* on 20 June 1993. *Gavin Morrison*

081

Left:
Its Construction subsector decals notwithstanding, No 60 005 *Skiddaw* is seen on Coal duty, heading a train of empties past the level crossing at England Lane, Knottingley, on the Drax/ Eggborough–Gascoigne Wood MGR circuit, on 25 January 1994. *Gavin Morrison*

Right:
Nearly at the end of the long climb from Newport to Ebbw Vale, No 60 096 *Ben Macdui* slowly passes Cwm with one of the three Sunday-afternoon trains up the valley on 20 June 1993. *Gavin Morrison*

Left:
Another view of No 60 096 *Ben Macdui*, this time passing Agecroft, on the outskirts of Manchester, with a GMC 'Binliner' train for Dean Lane on 19 June 1992. *Gavin Morrison*

Right:
The Grassington branch lost its regular passenger services on 22 September 1930 and goods on 9 August 1969. However, the branch remains open as far as Swinden Quarry and is now owned by Tarmac, although on 30 July 1992, when this photograph was taken, the quarry was owned by Tilcon. No 60 095 *Crib Goch* hauls a loaded train from the quarry heading for Hull Dairycoates; it is passing Embsay Junction, where the branch joined the now closed through line along Wharfedale. Visible in the background (right) is Embsay, nowadays the southern terminus of the Embsay & Bolton Abbey Steam Railway.
Gavin Morrison

Right:
In the days before the Bedford–Bletchley line received serious attention from Network Rail No 60 009 *Carnedd Dafydd* passes the high chimneys of the brickworks at Stewartby with a stone train for Bletchley on 18 June 1993. *Gavin Morrison*

Petroleum subsector

Left:
Seen from the ring road at Scunthorpe on 4 April 1996, No 60 053 *John Reith* heads a short rake of empty steel wagons towards the station, while in the background a coal train for the steelworks' unloading terminal waits to depart behind a Loadhaul-liveried Class 56. *Gavin Morrison*

Above:
The popular photographic location of Caister Road, Melton Ross, is the setting for this picture of No 60 003 *Christopher Wren* heading train 6T26, the 15.04 Immingham–Scunthorpe ore working, towards Barnetby on 17 July 1996. *Gavin Morrison*

Above:
The bridge carrying the M62 over the East Coast main line at Heck (where in 2001 a Land Rover would leave the road and land on the line, causing a disastrous accident) can be seen on the left of this 23 March 1995 photograph, featuring No 60 053 *John Reith* heading south with empty tanks from Hunslet to Lindsey. On the right of the picture, in Plasmor's yard, can be seen Class 56 No 56 051, together with the local shunter. *Gavin Morrison*

Below:
No 60 054 *Charles Babbage* would be the last of the class to retain the Petroleum subsector decals. It is seen here heading south at Hellifield with train 6E49, the 08.55 Kirkby Thore–Milford empty gypsum working, on 17 December 2005. *Gavin Morrison*

Coal subsector

Left:
Numerically the first of the class to be allotted to the Coal subsector was No 60 004 *Lochnagar*, seen at Doncaster Works' open day on 13 May 1990. Based initially at the Railway Technical Centre at Derby, it also spent periods at Toton and Immingham for crew training before finally entering traffic on 3 November 1991. *Gavin Morrison*

Right:
Super-power for train 6M17, the 17.45 Stourton–Peak Forest working, on 22 June 1995 as it passes the site of the former Lancashire & Yorkshire steam shed at Wakefield Belle Vue behind Nos 60 061 *Alexander Graham Bell* and 60 015 *Bow Fell*. *Jason Rogers*

Below:
MGR trains pass between Gascoigne Wood and Monk Fryston on 2 February 1994. The loaded train is headed by No 60 004 *Lochnagar*, while the empties have Class 56 No 56 005 at their head. Gascoigne Wood pit, since closed, is just to the right of the picture. *Gavin Morrison*

Above right:
Another view of No 60 061 *Alexander Graham Bell*, this time heading an unidentified stone train from the Peak Forest area round the sharp curve at Rotherham Masborough on 13 April 1994. *Gavin Morrison*

Right:
An empty steel train from Shotton to South Wales, headed by No 60 092 *Reginald Munns*, passes Wrexham under stormy skies on 25 February 1995. *Gavin Morrison*

TIVOLI INN
TIVOLI INN
Marston's
ALES FOOD POOL
John Cotton
061

092

60071
071

058

Above left:
No 60 071 *Dorothy Garrod* leaves Blackburn heading west with a Padiham–Workington train on 11 June 1992. *Paul Corrie*

Left:
Presenting no problem for No 60 048 *Saddleback*, a loaded GMC 'Binliner' train from Pendleton to Dean Lane climbs the 1½ miles at 1 in 59/47 to Miles Platting, Manchester, on 11 June 1992. *Paul Corrie*

Above:
Passing through Olive Mount Cutting, which must be one of the most impressive in the country, No 60 045 *Josephine Butler* heads a loaded MGR train from Glasson Dock, on the outskirts of Liverpool, to Fiddler's Ferry power station, near Warrington. The photograph was taken on 20 August 1994. *Gavin Morrison*

Unbranded

Left:
During their relatively short careers to date the Class 60s have witnessed significant upheavals in the railway industry. As already described, in preparation for privatisation Railfreight's subsectors were replaced in the mid-1990s by three 'shadow' freight companies, each with its own identity, though all three would ultimately form part of EWS. As a result of all these changes a number of Class 60s, having lost their original decals, ran for a time without any logos whatsoever. One such locomotive, seen passing Lenton West Junction, near Nottingham, on Saturday 20 November 1999 with the 11.37 Kingsbury–Humber/Lindsey empty tanks, was No 60 069, at that time still named *Humphry Davy*. *Gavin Morrison*

Below:
Originating from the site of Frickley Colliery, where a considerable quantity of coal remained on the surface after closure, a loaded coal train waits to join the main line just south of Moorthorpe as No 60 028 *John Flamsteed* heads south with a heavy steel train on 2 May 1997. *Gavin Morrison*

Above:
With vestigial blue and yellow markings (by the cab door) giving a clue as to its Construction subsector origins, No 60 010 *Pumlumon / Plynlimon* stands at the head of a Redland ballast train automatically discharging its load at Bradley Junction, to the east of Huddersfield, on 13 June 1994.
Gavin Morrison

Right:
On 11 February 2002 train 6E17, the 11.56 from Peak Forest, arrives at Hunslet Balm Road before reversing into the discharge sidings (nowadays occupied by a Freightliner servicing depot). At the head of the train is No 60 095, formerly *Crib Goch*.
Gavin Morrison

Loadhaul

Above left:
Loadhaul's black livery was possibly the most impressive to be applied to the Class 60s. No 60 025, formerly *Joseph Lister*, gleams in autumn sunshine as it heads an empty ore train from Scunthorpe through Immingham Docks on the afternoon of 23 November 1996. *Gavin Morrison*

Left:
Formerly named *Moel Fammau*, No 60 008 *Gypsum Queen II* heads train 6M46, the 10.43 Redcar–Hardendale empty lime hoppers, seen from the lifting bridge near Tees Yard, on 25 June 2003. On 11 April 2006 this locomotive would be further renamed as *Sir William McAlpine*. *Gavin Morrison*

Above:
Heading north on the former Glasgow & South Western main line on 28 April 1998, No 60 025 approaches New Cumnock with a train of empty MGR wagons heading for Falkland Road Yard, near Ayr. Renamed *Caledonian Paper* on 29 August 1999, this locomotive was to spend 11 months out of traffic after colliding with No 60 085 in Llanwern yard in November 2000. *Gavin Morrison*

Above:
Three members of the class — Nos 60 050, 60 064 and 60 070 — had Loadhaul stickers applied to their existing Railfreight triple-grey livery. Passing Gascoigne Wood Colliery, No 60 064 *Back Tor* approaches the crossing at Hagg Lane with train 6D42, the 15.33 Leeds Hunslet–Lindsey empty tanks, on 9 February 2001. *Gavin Morrison*

Below:
Late-autumn sunshine catches No 60 070 *John Loudon McAdam* passing through Immingham Docks with an ore train for Frodingham, Scunthorpe, on 23 November 1996. Evidence of the area's petrochemical industry is clearly visible on the skyline. *Gavin Morrison*

Above:
The first of a sequence of pictures devoted to No 60 059 *Swinden Dalesman*, which was the first Class 60 to receive Loadhaul livery. Here the locomotive heads southwest past Saltley on the outskirts of Birmingham with a loaded Lackenby-Llanwern steel slab train during August 2003. *John Turner*

Right:
On 25 June 2004 *Swinden Dalesman* makes a fine sight heading train 6E09, the 10.27 Margam–Lackenby empty steel working, just north of Rotherham Masborough, where it is about to join the main line from Sheffield, having come via the 'back road'. *Gavin Morrison*

Above:
By 2006 No 60 059 *Swinden Dalesman* was the last of the class to retain Loadhaul livery without the addition of EWS stickers. On 7 June it was photographed passing Welbeck, near Normanton, with train 6M17, the 10.18 Leeds Stourton–Peak Forest empty RMC hoppers, which would have worked in loaded as the 6E17 (03.54 from Peak Forest). Currently this is the only regular booked freight to use the line through Dewsbury. *Gavin Morrison*

Below:
No 60 059 heads down the Midland main line at Cossington, just north of Leicester, with train 6M87, the 11.07 Ely–Peak Forest empty RMC hoppers, on 6 June 2006. *Gavin Morrison*

Above:
On 2 June 2006, having taken the empty RMC hoppers to Peak Forest as the 10.18 from Stourton, No 60 059 takes the loaded train from the quarry to the sidings ready for their next journey before returning to the refuelling point. *Gavin Morrison*

Below:
At the time of writing No 60 059 continues to retain Loadhaul livery without EWS branding. This picture shows it passing the lake just to the east of Horbury Junction, between Healey Mills and Wakefield Kirkgate, on 1 December 2006 with the 09.30 Roxby–Northenden empty GMC 'Binliner'. *Gavin Morrison*

Mainline

Below:
Only three members of the class — Nos 60 011, 60 044 and 60 078 — received the attractive blue livery of Mainline. Here an immaculate No 60 044 *Ailsa Craig* makes a cautious departure from the Oxcroft Washery (now closed) with a loaded MGR train for Toton yard on 25 July 1996. *Gavin Morrison*

Right:
Hauling a rake of empty MGR wagons to Oxcroft Washery on 25 July 1996, No 60 044 *Ailsa Craig* is seen from a footbridge between Hall Lane Junction and Seymour Yard to the east of Barrow Hill. The complex of lines in this area is now hardly used. *Gavin Morrison*

Below:
No 60 011 lost its *Cader Idris* nameplates for the first time in January 1996, but they were reaffixed in October 1996, then removed again in March 1997. The locomotive is seen passing Avonmouth Docks at the head of the Hallen Marsh–Furzebrook LPG tanks in July 1996. *John Turner*

Right:
On 31 March 1999 train 6E06, the 10.00 Bredbury–Roxby GMC 'Binliner', is seen between Thornhill and Healey Mills Yard headed by No 60 044 *Ailsa Craig*, by now covered in limestone dust after working in the Peak District. *Gavin Morrison*

Below:
After running round using the loop No 60 078 pulls away from Sevington on 14 March 2003 with the Stud Farm–Hothfield grit train. Formerly *Stac Pollaidh*, the locomotive had by now lost its name. In the background can be seen the new high-speed Channel Tunnel Rail Link. *Brian Stephenson*

Right:
The majority of Class 60s allotted to Mainline had the new company's logo applied to their existing Railfreight colours. No 60 088 *Buachaille Etive Mor* passes through the cutting at Hasland, just south of Chesterfield on the up goods line, heading train 6M42, the 14.00 Peak Forest–Washwood Heath loaded RMC hoppers, on 1 May 1997. *Gavin Morrison*

Below:
An empty steel train from Llanwern to Lackenby passes Cargo Fleet behind No 60 086 *Schiehallion* on 25 June 2003. *Gavin Morrison*

murco
Mainline

Left:
A light covering of snow lies on the ground as No 60 075 *Liathach*, descends the 1-in-105 gradient from Marsden to Huddersfield at the head of train 6E06, the Bredbury–Roxby GMC 'Binliner', passes Golcar on 2 March 2001.
Gavin Morrison

Below left:
Alexander Dock Junction, Newport, is the setting for this picture of the colourful 6B33 (13.42 Theale–Robeston empty Murco tanks) heading west on 22 February 2003 behind No 60 077, formerly *Canisp. Jason Rogers*

Above:
On 17 October 2003 train 6M52, the 10.16 Drax–Newbiggin gypsum working, approaches Appleby station behind No 60 076, which had lost its *Suilven* nameplates in January 1997. At the end of the up platform can be seen the water column used by steam specials running over the Settle & Carlisle line. *Gavin Morrison*

Centre left:
On 16 February 2001, due to the rebuilding of Leeds City station, train 6D72, the 11.32 Hull Dairycoates–Rylston (Swinden Quarry) working, was diverted via Burton Salmon and Stourton. No 60 072 is seen hauling the impressive consist past Stourton Freightliner Terminal, on the southern outskirts of Leeds.
Gavin Morrison

Left:
Another impressive train, sadly no longer running, was the Furzebrook–Hallen Marsh LPG tanks, shown negotiating the sharp curve of the triangle at Dr Days Junction, Bristol, during March 1996, with No 60 083 *Shining Tor* in charge. *J. Turner*

60015
TRANSRAIL
Bow Fell

Transrail

Left:
Created, along with Loadhaul and Mainline, as a prelude to privatisation, the Transrail 'shadow' freight company was formally launched at Arpley Yard, Warrington, on 29 August 1994. Unlike the other two companies it chose to retain the tri-tone grey used latterly by Railfreight, but with the addition of the logo seen here on the side of No 60 015 *Bow Fell*. Also in attendance were Class 37/5 No 37 509 and Class 56 No 56 099. *Gavin Morrison*

Below left:
Minus its original *Bleaklow Hill* nameplates, No 60 081 passes Walton, just south of Wakefield, with train 6E06, the Bredbury–Roxby GMC 'Binliner', on 18 August 1998. Repainted in lined Great Western green, this locomotive would be renamed as *Isambard Kingdom Brunel* at Old Oak Common on 5 August 2000, thereafter becoming the class's 'celebrity' locomotive.
Gavin Morrison

Above right:
The grass growing freely in the yard at Springs Branch, Wigan, adds colour to this picture of No 60 045 *Josephine Butler* awaiting its next duty on 12 July 1996.
Gavin Morrison

Centre right:
Photographed on 1 June 1996, train 6M19, the 11.12 Jarrow–Stanlow empty tanks, heads south near Hest Bank behind No 60 056 *William Beveridge*. *Gavin Morrison*

Right:
In misty light on 22 December 1998 train 6M05, the 09.30 Roxby–Northenden GMC 'Binliner', headed by No 60 034 *Carnedd Llewelyn*, arrives at Healey Mills Yard for a crew change.
Gavin Morrison

Left:
Paddock Cutting, to the west of Huddersfield, on the Standedge route, has always been one of the author's favourite photographic locations. The first of two views recorded from this spot features train 6E06, the 10.00 Bredbury–Roxby GMC 'Binliner', heading east down the 1-in-105 gradient on 6 September 2001 behind No 60 096 *Ben Macdui*. *Gavin Morrison*

Right:
Formerly *Alexander Graham Bell* but by now unnamed, No 60 061 heads west up the gradient through Paddock Cutting on 3 May 2006 with train 6M22, the 11.20 Leeds Hunslet–Tunstead empty cement tanks. *Gavin Morrison*

Left:
Taken on 5 October 1999 from the road bridge just to the north of Fitzwilliam station, on the Wakefield Westgate–Doncaster main line, this picture shows No 60 055 *Thomas Barnardo* at the head of train 6E06, the 10.00 Bredbury–Roxby GMC 'Binliner'. *Gavin Morrison*

Above:
Despite having Transrail lettering applied No 60 066 *John Logie Baird* somehow managed to retain its original Coal subsector decal (albeit on one side only) — the only member of the class to feature this combination. Ready to head south with an MGR train, the locomotive is seen at Stafford station on 16 July 2001. *Gavin Morrison*

Right:
On 15 August 1995 Transrail's No 60 005 *Skiddaw* shunts wagons at the Blue Circle Cement depot at Dewsbury, which is situated to the south of the town on a short branch from Dewsbury East Junction, on the Calder Valley main line. The wagons would return to Earle's Sidings in the Hope Valley by what was then virtually a daily working. This still runs, albeit on an 'as required' basis, as train 6M89, the 09.53 departure, but is now operated by Freightliner. *Gavin Morrison*

EWS

Above:
Formed in 1996 to take over BR's trainload freight companies, EWS took some time deciding upon a livery. During this time a number of overhauled locomotives were released to traffic in undercoat. Among these was a single Class 60, No 60 022, seen here at Caister Road, just east of Barnetby, with an Immingham–Scunthorpe ore train on 4 April 1996. *Gavin Morrison*

Left:
Another view of No 60 022 at Caister Road, Barnetby, heading an empty Scunthorpe–Immingham ore train earlier the same day.
Gavin Morrison

Above:
Eventually EWS decided to adopt the livery of deep red and gold used by parent company Wisconsin Central in the USA, and from April 1996 Class 60s started to appear in these colours. In ex-works condition No 60 051, by now minus its *Mary Somerville* nameplates, passes Stenson Junction at the head of train 6M57, the 08.29 Lindsey–Kingsbury loaded bogie tanks, on 15 May 1997. *Gavin Morrison*

Right:
No 60 001, with its distinctive blue-backed *The Railway Observer* nameplate, pauses in the centre road at Carlisle on 28 August 2002 with a late-afternoon up 'Enterprise' service, which includes empty china-clay wagons returning from Irvine to Burngullow.
Gavin Morrison

Above:
The gypsum workings to Newbiggin over the Settle & Carlisle line were worked by Class 60s for many years, but more recently Class 66s seem to have taken over in summer. No 60 026 heads the empty wagons constituting train 6E13, the 12.40 Newbiggin–Milford, past Waitby on 29 December 2003. *Gavin Morrison*

Below:
Journey's end for train 6M22, the 11.20 from Leeds Hunslet, as it approaches Tunstead Quarry at Great Rocks behind by No 60 069 *Slioch* (which name had been transferred from No 60 087 in 2004) on 2 June 2006. *Gavin Morrison*

Right:
Batley in West Yorkshire was once a busy railway centre but is now reduced to two through lines, with only one booked freight per day, which heads east in the early morning. No 60 031 *ABP Connect* climbs the 1-in-138 gradient to the summit in Morley Tunnel with the heavy 6E17 03.46 Tunstead–Leeds Hunslet RMC stone train on 5 July 2004. *Gavin Morrison*

Below:
The Colne Valley, which runs west from Huddersfield to Marsden, abounds in photogenic locations, with viaducts, mills, the canal and old houses. Seen from the south side of the valley above Slaithwaite, No 60 085 *Mini — Pride of Oxford* crosses Slaithwaite Viaduct as it climbs the 1-in-105 gradient to Marsden at the head of train 6M05, the 09.30 Roxby–Northenden GMC empty 'Binliner', on 16 November 2005. *Gavin Morrison*

Above:
High in the Peak District hills, No 60 022 heads train 6H57, the 12.36 Ashburys–Dowlow empty box wagons, past Harpur Hill on 2 June 2006. *Gavin Morrison*

Right:
The very late-running Lindsey–Eggborough loaded bogie tanks passes Knottingley station headed by No 60 062 on 21 October 2004. *Gavin Morrison*

Below:
Heading a rake of ex-National Power JHA wagons, No 60 047 heads west past Warrington Monks sidings toward Fiddler's Ferry power station on 30 October 2001. *Gavin Morrison*

Above:
The Class 60s were once regular visitors to Cornwall, but by the time of writing (2007) appearances were rare. Here No 60 051 stands alongside Par station at the head of train 6M72, the 16.58 St Blazey–Cliffe Vale china-clay working, on 20 July 1999. *Paul Corrie*

Below:
On 15 February 2003 No 60 097 *ABP Port of Grimsby & Immingham* heads along the Erewash Valley line at Stonebroom with train 6V40, the 04.55 Lackenby–Llanwern, diverted due to engineering works between Clay Cross and Derby. *Gavin Morrison*

Left:
Photographed during June 2006 at Harrowden Junction, just north of Wellingborough, the 13.15 Colnbrook–Lindsey empty oil tanks heads north with No 60 038 *AvestaPolarit* in charge. *John Turner*

Left:
Train 6T83, a special 11.00 Tyne Yard–Doncaster empty ballast working for Network Rail, heads south through Sherburn-in-Elmet on 9 October 2006 behind No 60 023. *Gavin Morrison*

Below:
In April 2000, to celebrate the publication's 500th issue, EWS renumbered No 60 016 *RAIL Magazine* as 60 500. Seen in its new guise and in EWS livery on 31 October 2005, the locomotive heads train 6D48, the loaded limestone from Rylston Quarry to Heck, through the Gascoigne Wood complex near Selby. *Gavin Morrison*

Right:
After more than 10 years in EWS ownership a number of the operational Class 60s have still not been repainted in EWS livery. In 2006 the company decided to apply large 'EWS' stickers to non-EWS-liveried locomotives, as demonstrated by No 60 060 on 2 June 2006. *Gavin Morrison*

Below:
Currently the only Mainline blue-liveried Class 60 in service, No 60 044 is seen in the quarry sidings at Peak Forest on 9 June 2006. *Gavin Morrison*

Above:
The last two former Loadhaul-liveried members of the class in service by 8 June 2006 were Nos 60 007 and 60 059, and the former is shown catching the late-afternoon sunshine at Weaver Junction as it heads north, running early with train 6C73, the 16.15 Bescot–Carlisle. *Gavin Morrison*

Above right:
On 10 April 2006, running about 2½ hours late behind No 60 034 *Carnedd Llewellyn*, train 6E17, the 03.46 Tunstead–Leeds Hunslet RMC stone working, passes through Dewsbury, climbing towards the summit in Morley Tunnel. This is currently the only booked freight through Dewsbury and normally passes at around 06.45am, thereby restricting photography to the summer months. *Gavin Morrison*

Right:
On 3 June 2006 train 6M22, the 11.20 Leeds Hunslet–Tunstead coasts down the gradient between Diggle and Saddleworth behind No 60 060, complete with EWS sticker and still bearing its original name, *James Watt*. *Gavin Morrison*

W H SHAW
W.H. SHAW & SON LTD
EWS
60 060

British Steel

Left:
In July 1997 two members of the class, Nos 60 006 and 60 033, received this very attractive blue livery to the order of British Steel. On 14 September, two months after repaint, No 60 033 *Tees Steel Express* still looks immaculate approaching Mirfield, with Heaton Lodge Junction in the background, at the head of train 6E41, the 12.53 Blackburn–Lackenby empty Ferrywagons. *Gavin Morrison*

Above:
Despite their dedicated livery, the British Steel Class 60s were not confined to Metals duties. With the telecommunications mast on Emley Moor barely discernible through distant stormclouds, No 60 033 *Tees Steel Express* catches the sun as it heads north past Welbeck, near Normanton, on 16 February 1999 with train 6D08, the 10.21 Drax–Newbiggin gypsum working. *Gavin Morrison*

Corus

Above:
After British Steel was taken over by Corus the blue livery applied to Nos 60 006 and 60 033 was replaced Corus silver. No 60 033, seen here at Marsden on 16 December 2005 with train 6E06, the 10.00 Bredbury–Roxby GMC 'Binliner', retained its *Tees Steel Express* nameplates. *Gavin Morrison*

Right:
In immaculate condition, No 60 033 *Tees Steel Express* heads south through the closed Rotherham Masborough station with a train of steel slabs for Corby or Llanwern on 20 August 2001.
Gavin Morrison

Great Western

In the summer of 2000 No 60 081 was plucked from relative obscurity, being outshopped in lined Great Western green livery, complete with brass cabside numbers, and renamed *Isambard Kingdom Brunel* at Old Oak Common open day on 5 August. (The choice of locomotive was dictated by that depot's steam-era shedcode, 81A.) In this guise it was to become something of a celebrity, its movements being widely recorded, but regrettably its exploits would be curtailed by a major engine failure early in 2005.

Above:
On 9 June 2003 No 60 081 passes through third-rail territory at Charing with the Stud Farm–Hothfield grit train, which had left Hither Green at 09.40.
Brian Stephenson

Left:
On 20 April 2004 'IKB' was in charge of train 6E06, the Bredbury–Roxby GMC 'Binliner', seen nearing the end of its journey over the Pennines as it climbs the 2-mile 1-in-93 Gunners Bank from Keadby lifting bridge to Scunthorpe station. On this section of line is Scotter Road (or Frodingham) Viaduct, which had 85 arches of 30ft span but which in the years 1910-12 was partly filled in to form an embankment.
Gavin Morrison

Right:
With No 60 081 at its head, this time on 23 April 2004, the 6M17 Leeds Stourton–Peak Forest climbs the 1-in-100 gradient from Sheffield Midland to Dore & Totley at Millhouses, where the Midland Railway steam shed was once situated. *Gavin Morrison*

Below:
Photographed on 9 September 2004 at the head of train 6M17, the 10.18 empty limestone working from Leeds Stourton to Peak Forest, a work-stained No 60 081 has just emerged from the 2 miles 182yd of Cowburn Tunnel (between Edale and Chinley Junction), built between 1888 and 1892 by the Midland Railway. *Gavin Morrison*

Left:
60 001.

Below left:
60 097.

Bottom left:
60 048.

Below right:
60 060.

Centre right:
60 098. (This nameplate is on display in the Brush offices at Loughborough.)

Bottom right:
60 008.

Nameplates